lunatic

Lunatic

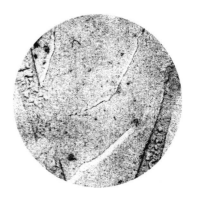

POEMS BY

Crystal Williams

Michigan State University Press
East Lansing

⊗ The paper used in this publication meets the minimum requirements of ANSI/NISO z39.48–1992 (R 1997) (Permanence of Paper).

Michigan State University Press
East Lansing, Michigan 48823–5245

Printed and bound in the United States of America.

08 07 06 05 04 03 02   1 2 3 4 5 6 7 8 9 10

LIBRARY OF CONGRESS CATALOGING-IN-PUBLICATION DATA

Williams, Crystal, 1970–
Lunatic: poems / by Crystal Williams.
   p. cm.
ISBN 0-87013-642-9 (alk. paper)
1. Title.
PS3573.I448414   L86   2002
811'.54 — DC21

2002151113

Cover design by Ariana Grabec-Dingman, Harriman, NY
Book design by Valerie Brewster, Scribe Typography, Port Townsend, WA

Visit Michigan State University Press on the World Wide Web at:

www.msupress.msu.edu

In memory of my mother

Marilyn Theresa Gumbleton (1937–2000)

who taught me what I know of forgiveness
and courage.

and for

E. Catherine Falvey,
Kenneth Anderson McClane Jr.,
and Marilyn McCormick.

Your generosity is overwhelming,
and often irreconcilable.

Contents

part one

part two

part three

LUNATIC

If we do not dare everything, the fulfillment of that prophecy,
recreated from the Bible in song by a slave, is upon us:
God gave Noah the rainbow sign,
No more water, the fire next time!

JAMES BALDWIN

part one

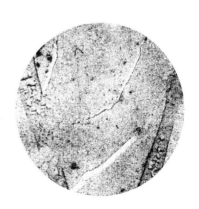

Poem for Rosa

Africa roams your face. Dark
& delicious. She prospers,
still, even though. Gambia riots
your face. People know at once
your tribe, its customs & failures. Stop,
speak your father's tongue
& although you don't know it
well, you smile. Sister.
Brother. What rumbling that must be. I look on
not knowing & knowing at once the possession
licking your ears. Africa. I hear her
footsteps in sculpture: This man is Nigerian,
look to his head, Ibo. His lips speak it
fully. I detect, piece what I can, map—hindered.
No nearer than the salon
where Ghana races across my scalp,
fingers lean & moist & quickly welcomed.
Awura-Abena's *eh's* slip down my back
so close. But that ends too,

& I, the adopted daughter—Black
father dead, white mother thriving—am left
without such certainties,
with only rumors, every now & again.

There is nothing about my face
except evidence & longing,
longing & these few homeless stories.

Friendly's

"Don't leave two dollars! Shit he ain't barely do nothing,"
she crackles, rancid language challenging even me,
three tables away though I was only looking for a burger,
some fries, a refillable Coke. I once waited tables
for women like this & so look up, want to catch her
defiant eyes cast over the whole as she assesses herself
by such ugly reflection. & me there. Whispering excuses
to my white co-workers, refusing to wait on "Little Africa,"
arguing a hostess who thought I'd be honored to serve my people.
& yes, the near empty pockets at night end, the inordinate running
for water, more ice, cubed not crushed, the "Can't you hear?
I said *baked* potato," the back & forth, our sour scuffle
for power. How fattened & parched my tongue grew
with explanation. & oh, God, what I wanted to say: here,
here I stand, the rose stripped of its thorn, the black
stripped of its nigger.

This Side of the Water

for Amadou Diallo & the Many Thousands

Amadou,
your mother is lovely.
She's been on TV fighting
for you. At first, she wore Africa,
a reddening eruption. Then it was West —
a skirt & blouse fixed stiffly on her, she stiffly in them.
The transition troubled me.
I wonder if someone, some strategist advised her:
here, we wear reasonable clothing. Probably
not like that, though. Probably mentioned her beauty
& pain; something about allowing for Americans' simplicity.
I want her to understand we are not all like this,
all of the time. This is our burden & I might show her it,
lift my blouse & point to the veins. Brother,
you are gone. Another Black man this side of the water succumbed
to the shot, the drag, the beat. I wonder if you'd been warned.
Riches, yes. & travesties. But more: this country does something dark
& dank to brown men. No matter money. They walk differently
with time. Some say the age of a man dictates the bop
in his step. But the bop does not leave, it only gets mauled,
becomes heavy under foot, sucks the body down.
Perhaps, had the cops seen your walk they would have known
you were not of here, the burdens not a shroud across your shoulders.
But that didn't happen & you were in that hall where it was dark & poor
in the Bronx which is dark & poor. & so, you were shot
many times, each time a renewed travesty. & we are left
with images of you in pictures & with your mother
to wonder. Had we passed on the street,

I may well have looked the other way,
ignored your bopping, skinny, smiley self, feigning blindness,
walking stiffly, without remorse. That might have been me
in contradiction. Shuffling beside you, impervious as I will need to be
in another several months, another brother dead, another bop gone.

On Cops & Color

DETROIT (1987)

Julani was driving his dad's Jag.
Methuselah wasn't so old, we laughed.
"You *shoulda* been stopped
for driving that thing!"

OHIO (1991)

Everyone knows if you're black,
don't get stopped in Ohio — especially
not speeding, which we weren't.

Those flashing lights panicked our eyes,
made our hearts pound like prey.
The Trooper's inquisition tattered
our middle class quilts —
his mouth: a thousand nesting moths.

One mile down the road he stopped us again.
Saul's five foot five inches grew into an
escaped convict from Florida who was six
foot two until the radio-voice told the Trooper
people cannot conjure themselves
into criminals with bigger bones.

D.C. (1993)

I am guilty. These are not my people,
them with their narrowing eyes & slouched pants
& sitting on stoops & go-go bands. But, then,
there was Philip & something not unlike love.

NEW YORK (1995)

It hit me in Chinatown, where I was lost
amid a sea of color: Cops know where they are.
Eric got shot in the back
by his blue brother, undercover uniform
too authentic.

T.V. (1998)

An exposé tells: the looming destruction
of a city, its fate bound in festering accusations
& tension thick as blood-pudding. Each side
to be believed — a little. Sometimes.

HERE (1998)

Julani blacked-out
our gibes.

Saul won't talk of Ohio,
says he is where he is.

Philip recounted strip searches:
his buttocks stretched, his balls
hanging. The fire looping him
was not desire & his eyes made me cry.

Eric sued the city & his brother.
His family & faith are gone.

I am guilty. Afraid
of the line I tow. I hope
when the day comes,
the cop will see me
& understand
whatever act I committed

could be no worse than this I carry,
than where I stand, teetering
between bones & brain.
I hope the jury considers this
was never my intention.

On Being a Good Minority: A Riff

Just yesterday your host called with a last minute invitation
to a gig & because you are only a $1.25 NYC subway token
& there are new/improved $1.50 tokens,
you accepted, but quick. So you show.
The gala, a benefit-type gig, is in full swing. Stale
breath over wine, cheeses galore
(phew, someone forgot their lactose pill),
whispers, certainly, drama of the highest caliber evidenced:
the plethora of oh-god-
what-the-fuck-is-this-idiot-in-front-of-me-saying poses.
No one is minding your bunny-behind.
So, you wander from boring yap to boring-er yap, finding,
finally, two characters communing with the punch bowl
& pontificating amenably. There. That's the ticket.
You do know these clowns. It's Tweety & Sylvester
(gigantisized & over their previous animosity)
seriously discussing the serious brilliance of California's
Anti-Affirmative Action Initiative. For a quick second
an image of heaven pops into your pee.
But just then they notice your inching-towards-them dark self
& before you know what's what
they've begun waddling your way like fat men at Sizzler—
you being a big ole all-you-can-eat prime rib roast.
So you ease back into the foyer all suave-like
but they're waddling after. So you slip outdoors.
Suddenly, Tweety & Sylvester are in
(an Adam12 moment)
hot pursuit, which is when you really start moving,
pedal to the metal—colored folks
are supposed to be able to run. But Tweety, happy bastard,
is getting the one up, calling out in a big ole deep
country-kitchen Mahalia Jackson voice

& you realize, Tweet's lisp is gone.
In fact, he's been to a speech pathologist.
But, you're hustling now with no pay-attention-time
'cause the fucker is quick, plus you've lost tabs on Sylvester.
& you realize staying alive is no joke,
is hard as hell & your legs ain't cutting it.
Just then Tweety cold turkeys, out of breath.
But sly Sly pops out of left field taking the lead
because although he converted to vegetarianism years ago
he just popped some LSD & right about now
you're looking like a sassy ass eggplant.
You dart & dash & carl lewis 'til you realize this silliness
is all some misunderstanding (a Clarence Thomas moment) —
you are all same-sided, which causes pause. You turn,
attempt explanation, which backfires 'cause
you trip, ass out (& up). To the grass you go.
Caught like a hooker in maximum security.
& right before you die you realize:

all the private schools
for intelligent children, the foreign language lessons,
the summer trips to Europe, the sat preparation course,
(okay, & then again the sat preparation course),
the ivy league tuition was all for naught.
& just as that left canine pierces your glute you think: God
damn, shoulda taken track.

The Shackle vs. The Chamber

for Mel

No.
No Greeks. No Romans. No
introductory commentaries, generalities.
Let the Smithsonian build a complex
to explain *Enslavement.* But this, no.
Some things do not require context:
the Holocaust Museum's cavernous memory;
a thousand shoes plummeting; the darkened faces
singing. The walled photos — an entire village
in flickering snaps of light. I too want a palpitating museum
chanting these eye-songs, these darkening, congealed hymns.
The world must know our gods. Waters remain seasoned. Show me
the slave ships' shackled & spooned. Show me. Show me
the corollaries, bright as shark teeth.

South Carolina: Tour,
Boone Hall Plantation, 1999

for Jackie & Cybele

I

Thought this trip south would be a sojourn.
But there is nothing certain here.
Just the picturescape: row of angel oaks — halo's hailing
God; long horse necks bent on grazing, Spanish moss dancing
a slow waltz or a two step here & there. Egrets perched
like plastic on ponds. Only the Big House,
so much smaller than my mind's cast, seems real.

There is the row, that red red row of nine brick houses
or maybe call them dwellings if a house
is a home, if a home is where your heart is
call them dwellings out of courtesy.

That red red row just front-left of the main house.
But, they too mean little. Only, once a woman must have
peered beyond a large drape of curtain, her eyes out & over
the gardened walk tracing those crimson walls, checking,
just making sure all remained as yesterday & before.

That is all, a glimmer of sight, no moans
appealing, no reconfiguring of my scattered bones,
no voices of my sinew & synapse
brethren. Solely this silence & slow tatter
of my never-been-south expectation.

II

In the gentleman's quarters — a room of wooden walls
& wooden floors creaky & ridden with confidence — hints linger:
ledgers, blueprints, stories long misunderstood & discarded.

We cram into this space, shuffle & pardon our selves elbows
& bent backs. Stop at the curio, peer in to see what persists.
Almost nothing. Except, here.

A one inch by one inch tag
numbered 604. I have seen these slave tags,
these number names before. Imagine them on leather about
black necks. When asked, the guide cannot say how many *servants*
worked this acreage, seventeen thousand in all,
more than twenty square city blocks. She points to the red bricks
try the servants' houses, usually someone's over there who would
know. But, no one, nothing. What was supposed to be here is gone.
The man who knows — gone. We complain.

How many	How
How many	When
Where	How long?

One hundred, one hundred slaves
would have lived on, worked a plantation this size,
the saccharine director offers under our disappearing eyes.
We are static, unmoved, undetermined. Still,
retreat, screams muffled, bound, taut, merciless.

The Others

CHICAGO, 1919: *"A colored boy swam across an imaginary segregation line. White boys threw rocks at him and knocked him off a raft. He was drowned. Colored people rushed to a policeman and asked for the arrest of the boys throwing the stones. The policeman refused."**

Every harsh word uttered rolled from his Black behind
like water off a duck. He was hard-headed as rocks,
had centipede-eyes, & could tell you math, english,
all types of encyclopedic fanciness.

V.J. ran knocked-kneed through the Belt
helloing everyone, conversing with Crazy Otis
like he was talking to Jesus, petting One-Eye-Edna's
mean-ass dog, Thunder.

Had a tongue sweet as the apple pies he loved,
Mornin' Mrs. so-and-so, haven't seen you at Daddy's sermon in awhile.
Then sure 'nough, Sunday, they'd come in a-winking.

"Verdell Jacob Collard," Momma'd say,
"boy, you gonna either be head of the NAACP or
dead one day, 'cause you are too fresh!"
Then they'd laugh, like two grown folks.

When we heard, we ran down to the water & searched him.
Coloreds & whites were screaming, spitting,
throwing every kind of thing. We snatched him up
& Ma & me found our way home with brother trailing,
eyes full of Crazy Otis & Thunder.

*"The Chicago Race Riots: July, 1919" Carl Sandburg. Harcourt Brace 1969

Tour for Troubled Youths: L.A. Morgue

Here, gangless & without battle
they long for their tribal corners & Red Bull.
Some willow, some shed, some root
as they shuffle past a burned body—
legs cast in perpetual motion.

In tongues, the dead shriek STOP!
like the church women
whose bodies jerked a holy garble
way back when.

Now, it's the Doctor's echoing: Lookit,
gangs killed her, she was ten, him, sixteen.
These two & that one & those four stacks,
this is all gang violence. They stare.
He stares back until eyes begin their flicker,
keeps his mouth moving, the tentacle in his throat
fevered, grasping, shrieking names, telling it all until
his tongue swells, until at least one of those children
hears too clearly old church women getting God.

911

Rise. It's come, the darkening locust.
For years we had heard tell.
Like children most of us
turned, ignored, dug our holes
& motes, let the bullies fortify
their trenches, mount defenses,
kick the sand. Now,
with one ground to be had,
it is easy to see a single life
is too much when it is yours
or your brother's or your neighbor's
neighbor. We are not children.
There will be war. Darkness.
We will beat it back,
drench it in fire until it falls
on bloodied, ashen knees.
& what will we have lost?
Besides bodies who knows
but to say there is always sand
to be kicked & someone to kick it back.
That we are so wide-eyed, still,
is miracle. In all ways, death,
silence. In all ways: beauty. From ash
rise the sparkling questions: today,
in the early hours, before you saw
what could be, what were you doing?
What had you done?

The Hats

for Rosa Parks

On TV, they have thought to be clever,
confined you to a bus,
back-light shining
the edges of your Sunday-hat,
that lime green conglomerate
wild as a child's squeal.
I imagine your feet swollen
round as Dizzy's cheeks
& stuffed into beige one inch pumps.
Your suit, a single breasted fuchsia,
flurries of scarf, a brooch handed down
from your mother & hers. You remind me
of the every-Sunday women. Miss Lily,
Miss Bert, Mrs. Rudolph Webster & their hats
perched like raging roosters — announcing,
as if all would be lost without such acts
of resistance & submission.
I saw you then: faith sturdy,
body not long for here,
the hats to be sent off,
wrapped & bound, delivered
upon a town's Good Will,
to be fingered & considered
out of context. I know you,
now,
like this:
makin' sweet potato pies sing,
smile barely there, thin arms reaching,
reconciling, black eyes insistent,
insisting on Sunday.

In Search of an American Language
(or, After Being Accused of "Coding")

I was born   Here
to a father who worked ford longer than
I have mused. I was born black & surplus
a uaw puritan
baby
momma worked herself
through school for her
bookish bilingual   speak
main street girl. These here is mine: platforms
afros vanderbilts p-funk & labelle the carpenters & dylan
roller-rinking to the jacksons five & solo
metal detectors reagan bush a cousin named clifford
who disappeared probably
in prison or dead.
Where be yours?   Tell it
clearly. When detroit was cracking
& motown long gone I was small spent
afternoons accessing
the down-
town library & summers abroad.
I was born   Here.
black & woman
fringed & expected
to read beyond
my grade. I navigate naked
without toga or fig
mythless & decoded.   america sings dastardly
& I in a rowdy off-key sass.
I was born in 1970 at 8:49 am & by no fault of my own am
a cusp-born libra a leo
rising bumrushing any language I can. I am

from Here. american.
& have been accused of speaking
in some translation
other than
this bedeviled tongue. & I know
all kinds. Shit. I know what is expected
of me. I know this: Here be our collective.

Miscommunication

An update meeting has been called.
Each student wants to know: who,
when. Covertly we assess the prospects,
our silent circuses & ghosts rooting.

I say: we need another white man
like we need another white man.

The white boys haw; shift themselves
as if they've got a wedgy,
long to rearrange their stuff;
think I'm crazy, misguided, or worse:
too shallow to understand the gravity
of where we are; want to think
I'm talking about quotas.

Of the ten writers in the department there are
only two: one black, one chicana, I offer.

Yes, right,
this *is* America, their eyes say.

Today historians ate dirt:
Thomas fucked Sally & her children.
Some of the white Jeffersons are legally black,
but they are not speakers of tongue, not kin.

The white boys shift their shit again.

At meeting end we've accomplished
nothing, have frustrated ourselves
with inevitability. I rise to leave with a tiring

tongue & body full with accommodation.
There is no place else to tuck, stash, squirrel.
Every nasty crevice I've got is exploding.

What I said
was you need (*a possessor of tongues*)
another white man
like you need (*a frickin' translating ghost buster*)
another white man, (*up in here*)
aaaaaaiiiiiiiiiiiiiiiiiiiiiiiiiaaaaaaaaaaaayyyy (*for your own good*)
aaaaaaiiiiiiiiiiiiiiiiiiiiiiiiiiaaaaaaaaaaaayyyy (*understand?*)

You

stand less than a foot from me, flipping your brilliant hair.
A strand catches my mouth, the lips which are glossed
& prettied. The world is a tire track. Here. This moment:
Snatch the hair from your scalp or let it float gently away.
My friend glances at me & I know it is in my eyes,
the brazen hefers, the tattle tells. My lips have been glossed
for one year & seven months. Dateless & ugly. I am not an apparition,
not a speck of light in the corner of your eye. I am a woman
& have a name, a life, a car, a cat who loves me. I have hair, too.
& could flip it but this is not a city for me. I am too black, I think,
too big, too much of something. What is this that women do? Sister,
the voice whispers, & I flash to a mountain, am in a forest
where bodies make no difference, where white or black
is full moon or sliver but giving light. This is so much work,
too much work today when I am alone & watching your myriad
sisters prancing, gulping at their lives, when I am alone
& have no faith or proof that my cup, too,
will one day dribble. It is too much to be big
& generous, to chant, "Sister, Sister: love." It is too much to wonder
at Beauty & the snarl of my heart. I have to have something. Right
now you are real & in front of me, your hair is in my mouth
& what I want is to finally say, "You, you, white girl,
keep your fucking hair to yourself."

Sculpture 101

Even when we don't try, we usually sculpt ourselves.
TODD MCGRAIN

I have audited this course in order to see
the curve of cheek to jaw, the way a hand flourishes air.
We discuss figurative movement, abstraction, post-modern
theory.

When others see strength in the broad strokes of abstraction,
I see the sadness of beauty confined.

On final assignment, my classmates are freed:
they paint & chisel, sculpt, rename. I layer clay
until a broad nose, dreadheaded woman emerges.

On final crit. the class circles my blue girl, observes
the smirk of her lips, the rabid dreads. *I wanted to study
solitude & rage: a peaceful face, a head fully frenzied.*

Does she have a name? they ask. *Yes.
Her name is Smile-like-you-know-something-good.*

Once home I'll raise her to the light & shout
the only abstraction I know: Look, Black
people, look at yourselves.
Look here at your blue Black selves & see.

Landscapes

Portland, OR

Spent morning silently walking the new neighborhood; to Saturday Market,
through Old Town, along the water, then on over to the juried art fair
where just about every other vendor is selling "spirit guides"
disguised as wrinkled black folk. I suppose we've always been

somebody's purveyor of spirit. But, since when have so many
white folks been so forthcoming? In the body
of an artist's statement, a Mississippian writes,
"when people see my work they expect me to be an old black man . . ."

& on & on about the time she spends with black kids
who are ready for any art to speak their name. I am made anxious
by her insistence. This is a morning of conflation
& I am unable to discern what's what.

For example: all the black men here are attached to white women.
They ignore me. I them. We're two dogs sniffing the same crusty tree;
our scents familiar & disturbing, undeniable. Better to keep away,
avoid the fight. Somehow today

our circling is especially hurtful. So, I ignore the brothers & hide-
out in the should-be-black white woman's booth where I heave
myself at the canvases, attempt to access the abstracted faces
which are all black & only black. No wonder

there is so much abstraction, I think, she colors us
in translation. Black faces for white folks to buy. How simple
& small I've become. I ache to say: render as you like. Yet, can
not. My imagination places her before an empty canvas, yearning

to paint my folks — struggling with the language in their faces.
She might have stood before the Balinese rain forests, enraptured,
yet uncertain of the landscape. & so, most easy: to all the same shade
of green. But there should be a tiny dot of white, if we are to believe.

Conflation. I, too, force upon my brothers a language they may not speak.
But we are family & in the world our rifts don't matter. By her hand,
we are both made models, interchangeably silenced,
simply surrendered to the wall again & again.

On the Collection of Ethnic Memorabilia

It's a relatively new fad in TV history: thousands of folk
crammed into convention halls hoping to get their legacies appraised.

& so it is, almost always white, they stand, coveting,
waiting on their fortunes to be told. For the occasional lucky

bastard, the dusty moccasins great grand daddy "just always had"
but whose origins remain murky, the Boston breakfront, the ugly ass

estate sale print turn out to be worth mucho dinero, sometimes
mucho mucho dinero, as in buy a small house in Iowa dinero.

Mostly, the money is just enough to make their lives prettier. Maybe
they buy a new car or put some away for their kids' education.

Maybe they repaint the house a new shade of tan while thanking
great great auntie, that bohemian, extravagant collector. As it is,

I watch, a member of the rest of us, transfixed by possibility:
unless I win the lotto, I won't ever buy a signed Hurston

or an unsigned Hurston. Baldwin, too, is beyond my grasp.
Somehow I believe he'd be saddened by this. He would sense

who had read & loved & who had only procured. He might cry,
as I do, at this injustice. Probably, though, he'd be hopping mad

& write some beautiful dragon fire — upset
the entire book-collecting populous, force people to dust off

their collections & turn them in. Bearden would collage until his hands
were raw & the colors would be red & cayenne red & fire red.

Zora would hurumph & spit. Miles would piss. Under this circumstance,
Colored folk, gather you what remains. Our legacies,

these noble high roads, intangible & growing lesser with time,
these paths insurmountably overgrown & damned

overrated, are worthy for the gather, children. Children,
gather. Gather. Gather, you.

To Chloe from Crystal, with Love

When you were very little
not walking even, you were agreeable.
I could snatch you from your parents
& you'd cling. Although, you'd cling to most anybody, then.

After vacation, in a new year, new millennium,
after I had not seen you for some time,
I walked in & you howled a God-awful series of yelps,
your face turned pink then red & brighter still.
I was dismayed. Right then,
I thought of my Blackness
& Sharps Chapel where you had been,
where few Black folks live, I imagine.
I thought: this baby has just seen me
& is frightened by what she has seen.
What must I look like? A Black
hulk of creature standing at the door, stomping
mud from my feet. You were not to be calmed.

I've taken to visiting biweekly.
Now, you will let me hold you — briefly.
Mostly, you are impervious, a sweet smile
here & there. But running on your
new found legs is infinity intriguing.

Things are as they should be. Yet I worry.

As you grow you will find people bring with them the world.
With each person a different, gnarled mess.
I wonder if you saw mine, fear you will soon be unable to tell
which mess is yours & which are the worlds
people have thrust at you. I worry that somewhere

along the line you'll learn screaming is inappropriate.
Girl, I hope your good folks with their good hearts will teach you
the world operates in silence, the silent operate the world,
& your new lungs were our best hope.

To what place you goin', Girl?

Dunno. Suppose I oughta put my feet to the ground
& if it be unsteady & steady, cold & hot, it'll live
in me as it is. In this body. In this spine. This life
be where, friend, but here?

PART TWO

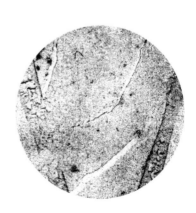

Home Sick

Living in Portland, Oregon is to live atop Mt. Hood
where it's cold as a witch's tit & unabashedly white.
In these parts, folk day-trip the mountain to do
God knows what, ski or hike, fuck up the habitat.
In Detroit, there's no nature outside of our own
unrelenting mess.

My students say this aversion to nature is a fault.
They misunderstand. I'm not averse to beauty.
In nature, our laws prove us stupid. Bears claim dens,
mountain lions, the rest. People have been mauled,
eaten for appropriating the habitat of others, suffer
for asking unanswerable questions, die from ignoring
the answers we've got. That is magic enough for me. Today,

I cowered, one of two black women, at the new year's
first faculty meeting. Someone bothered to ask how many
incoming students were black. Some eyebrows twitched
but our mouths maintained their grim press, quickly returned
to curricula, activities, how we might positively influence
our charges. All of us ignored the fat-ass elephant. & I tell you,
damned if I didn't hear the trees murmur & the wind wail, *two,
two*. & damned if I didn't think of home & wonder
if I'll ever be able to skulk back.

Home

for Jesse

There is something down there
not like your mother or father or a magnolia tree.
Nothing so beautiful. Some thing
other. Like the smell of day old onion
banging around a kitchen, mutating through the halls,
settling into the velvet sofa. It is like that, this thing.
I have been watching you full in its grip,
have wanted to shake it away, drag it into the sun
but have not known how or if such measures are appropriate.

Whatever is in the dank Tennessee air that so holds you
scares me just like a lover's midday sweats —
Sickle Cell running him to God; just like that skinned
onion that becomes dirty cat litter, day-old chicken fat,
a drain stuffed with sludge.

I would make my hands raw, I have made my hands
raw with trying to clean out the shit in my house. Mostly,
these days, I endure. Imagine some animal has succumbed
burrowed in the wall.

But that is my house. & Tennessee is in your eyes. Like my cat,
every motion sends you running. She to the kitchen-feed.
You to there & that thing you cannot name.

Why I am bothered by this, I cannot say. Perhaps it is
your calm acceptance: Tennessee is where you'll go. I am jealous.
There is no greedy, single-minded earth pulling at me.
There is no excuse so great as a state, a town, a family
for me. There is only my kitchen & raw hands,
digging about crudely.

Thirty

This is how it will be now. The emergencies
no longer dodging bill collectors, city issued
tire-boots, getting dumped, getting canned, the fire
alarms of identity lost & found, lost again.
To dismiss these would be to descend into the cobalt tunnel
& ignore the train, it's path & stops.
I could have been calm & quiet,
learning. I might have sat down, given my body to the roll,
heeded Momma who, although I did not ask, offered,
go into it fully, don't stay down too long, I'm here when you're ready.
I listened, mostly. Came out when I pleased. The ride was mine.
My questions: answered. But, here now,
language gathers anew & to emergencies a new meaning: Momma
in intensive care, tubes running around her island of a bed,
the archaic & obtuse beeping, bits of blood dried to her hand,
the slow suck of oxygen. Two liters of fluid enclose her heart
& the doctors, each day a new young man, pay homage, mark charts,
shake their heads perplexedly. I am alone this trip,
suddenly myself, faced with mother's eyes,
full of a language I do not want to learn from her,
this new, emerging woman
who has come too quickly, is overcome with fear.
Two weeks ago I thought I'd gotten over:
went on ahead down the damned tunnel,
didn't stay too long, escaped without devastation. Except
mother is another woman. & Goddamn it, time lied.
The answers I've gathered belong to silly questions. & here
now, I, too: new, reluctant woman.

From the Hospital, Hood

Portland, OR

My mother is dying & in the distance
the mountain hulks along the ridge, white, too big
for description. I stand upon an opposing hill.
Face to face, this mountain & I. Between us, the city
flattened. Something in me wants to count the houses,
the small blips of light that make pretty patterns,
divide that number by another unknown quantity,
figure how many humans down there live,
in near darkness, as orphans. Solace, then. People
continue. This is a new tribe to which I will belong
& I wonder if I will recognize them. Do they stand
braced against the smallest gust? Are their eyes full-up
with bewilderment & wild with unfulfilled stories?
Will they recognize me, these, my brethren? No,
my heart moans. No. Soon the mountain will be overtaken
& it will be me alone on a hill, facing the deep dark
above a city I do not know, full of a people who will never know
me. I should turn my back to it
now, return to Momma, remember it: perfectly
beautiful, crested yet gorged, hulking above the drudgery.

Bridge

In front of the Oncologists
my questions gather in little puckers,
slide along my tongue, expand,
reach for the specific — a name, a nature.
Even under such hard light I am not here,
am glancing at the room with a third eye:
the smallness, the sadness that drips & dips
the walls, the white of their coats,
the breaths etching along our throats.

We had talked about this moment over the years
as people talk about love, in generalities,
grand sweeps. If the time came my mother had faith,
she said, patting my cheek, wanted me to be the one,
"You'll know when. You'll know what."

Today they still do not have a name.
I want to keep her until the answers are clear,
resound. I want Time to do this work.
But Time does not comply & I am forced to say,
Let her go.

They draw the ventilator from her mouth & I turn,
turn on Lou Rawls, grasp her cold, swollen hand,
lower my head to her arm. The doctors & nurses are here.
My uncle is here. Daddy, though dead, is here.
Someone whispers, *You have to know this was the right thing.*
I imagine Daddy reaching down for her as I reach up.
I imagine her suspended between our two black hands —
between here & there, answering us both, her body
a perfect exclamation, a bright, white bridge.

Fumes

for Jimmy

What does it feel like, you ask. I am
a mishmash of bleak & garbled omens:
the girl forgotten at film-end because
the lovers are kissing; the padded room's
glaring glare & deepening hum; the woods
& dark, torpedoing; Miles & his back,
Jimi & his needle, Angela's fist; it is
to be in the world knowing however
many people are there, none belong to you;
to want so deeply your bones go cold
at night, you skin fulfilling its fallowness,
your tongue sour, bursting; death at an early age,
without its answers or its tunnel or even the damned
light, just dark, Love; it is darkness & meaninglessness
& there are no lips or kisses, no hands laying on,
only symbols: crying fetuses, maimed, masturbating men,
dead women cackling all coming at you in dream,
all piling their noise into one bone cold body;
it is every long moan ever written, a tome. I am.

Afterword

& to the house she wanted us to share
& to the nights in this new town
when she was alone — knowing no one
but the wind as it hurled itself at the walls:
I don't want to live with you. I don't want to feel
like I have to come over here all the time,
Momma. I have a life, you know.

What is left is her face, eyes reaching into the night.
Sometimes she'd mutter, *It's okay. I understand.*
Do what you have to do. Come when you want.
Sometimes she'd simply place her hand on my cheek.

I do not know where she went in those moments of my harshness
or how much of herself she was forced to leave behind
when she came back to face me, her chosen child,
her girl, once so soft. I thought this was hers to reconcile.

But, there are things in the air,
no matter how or where I go,
small ghosts I turn into each day,
a bump, a bruise, a remembrance
of my tongue & its lash,
my heart & its hard stare.

Benediction

The hair has to get washed, her things — sorted, the house
emptied; three boxes of stuffed animals for grandchildren
she anticipated, loved so much; my classes must be taught;
her papers read, shuffled, reported on; dinner had.
My explanations have grown concise, vary
from person to person — depending on their eyes:
My mother is no longer here. I am sure
I, too, am going to die — any minute. Fortune,
how much is a person allowed until it's time?
She did not suffer long: God. I say,
Mercy.   I am sipping the saucer:
found the old reel-to-reels, understand now
why she so relished Lou Rawls: he sounds like Daddy;
why she insisted on Christmas together:
fifteen boxes of my beaten, ragged toys, ten of ornaments;
pictures everywhere, in drawers; my poems, everywhere
in her wallet, in her backpack, tucked beneath the phone pad
so I would not find them & throw the God-awful things away.
So many things. Each a memory, now out in the world,
hastened away, to do some other good. So many
pictures. An empty box for each brother, over time
to be filled up, sent with, I don't know, some fragment, perhaps
another picture. Sweaters for nieces, stuffed rabbits
for grand nieces. A fire truck for small Ryan. These I can do.
Order the autopsy, the headstone, pay her taxes, light a candle. Pray.
I cannot replace her hands. I understand now
why she wanted me to marry, have children
but cannot reason these short tears, why I smile amid them,
laugh sometimes; cannot rationalize this sudden longing
for touch — people have been kind — & why, in these three months,
my vessel of a body, my dead wood of a body has begun to sprout
ruddy twigs. I cannot explain why I understand, no longer fear, love.

On Love & Solitude

after Rilke

They have come on suddenly, these eyes,
no longer popping & slick but coy, reticent even.
What is there to say about the wind
sassing us, the sun, the moon & their God
damned beating, the impending drought? What
is there to say to overshadow the whirlwind
here? Nothing of interest. Two months ago
I did not think at all, maybe a flutter,
a brief wind swooping the leaf, returning it
gently to its rest. Two months ago
I became a childless, motherless woman — full on;
to face the next thirty years alone. & what of it
but that everything has cleared — the way
solitude steam rolls the shit from our path.
It is late now
to hear the drum's fancy roll, to learn the protocols
of how to be with a man: what to do, the eyes
to paint. It is too late for me to learn sweet
vixen's secrets or sultry seductress smiles.
There are women I will never be.
I look to you, Man, say: time has gone,
I am only here for a spell & have been
left with sudden eyes to see her now,
that woman I might have painted you.
I might have said,
before it all seemed so impossible,
Man, you there, love me like this.

Still

If it is true about the waters
I am doomed. Oh, Man,
I dreamt you last night.
We were beyond my body,
had been years this way, like water & rock
at the base of a river. I dreamt your tongue
& it's sliver quickly over my collar bone,
a hundred times, each time like water
lapping the edges of a dark bank,
each time the silt grumbling at the disturbance,
each time the small fish living in the cool black,
waiting for their meal, thankful for your insistence.

Body Politic

What can I say. Time has done her number on me.
   I had forgotten the salt of our tongues & him, somewhere between
      reaching for manhood & having just gotten there. & I,
         still a girl, thirteen, big for my age. Yet

we sat on the park bench — legs & arms serpentine — tongues
      embroiled in fierce ritual. This must have been the first kiss.
         Not Dewayne in the basement, but a Spaniard in Madrid.
            The years have fattened up with consequence & misplaced

him, well. If I had my druthers, amid the rubble he'd stay.
      Of course, I can busy myself with answerable questions. What was he
         doing with me? Why did I join him, wasn't I bright?
            Words like pedophilia banter about.

But I am more selfish than that, absurdly so.
      What comes to me in this remembrance is
         Black, that thing I've become since the park, his tongue,
            the first escapade towards womanhood. I persist

a city where black men marry white women — without
      exception. My condemnations are swollen up from use. The Spaniard's
         a hiccup. How can I claim such ruthless politics, deny lovers
            their possibilities? Who am I to try when

once, as a girl who was only American,
      I kissed a man who was only Spaniard & thought: *I might be a traitor.*
         Those boundaries were so simple yet I could not deny
            such pleasure & so:

the sun across my back, his hands
      holding me there, superfluous,
         intent, the contortions my body made —
            that singular, naive yearning.

45

"U're Looking More & More Like a Comic Book Hero"

TY AVERY O'NEILL

Wolverine was cool, awesome
in a rugged sorta way. His hair, jet black
embers, danced a nasty funk two step,
& had moon-glow slitted eyes & a snarl
so sinister my thighs are still wobblin —
& wet & sweet. Wolverine was like *that*.

Had I been able I'da licked u offa them pages.
I'da swiveled my hips, tasted my lips,
murmured, *um um um. Damned.*
Can't keep from seein the pierce blue slash of u'r eyes,
from wondering at the funk in u'r hair, white
boy. Wanna cross these boundaries, drag my
palms on u'r skin, stick my fingers in u'r mouth & see
what'll become of 'em.

According to Kelli Fox

the monthly horoscope prophetess, Love is
oxygen, always in the air, waiting to be recognized,
captured like a lady bug & not flung or flicked away.
It's nearing, she writes. *Buy a new dress.*
According to the planets, this month Luck is my doll
or bitch. What are Libras to do? We crave peace
& harmony, weigh everything, ourselves mostly
(though, this for aesthetic reasons);
we want to be in love, are in love with love; suffer
amidst tangible beauty. Yes, yes, I say. True. & not.
Practically, my house is in order. But, ooh to be a Taurus
& ram my way through this drought. Not in my chart.
These are the planets given & I revolve, spin out of control,
grab for any seat back, the steady hope that something will give,
some love will get dislodged from its momma's hand, get lost,
wander my way. I am addicted. It is to hope, I know,
a way to remain among the linen drapes, chenille pillows,
the silvery brown walls I've taken such care to make just so.
The other seems so tedious. Toss, turn sheets, go months without
proper sleep, approach the answer as if it were the man of my dreams
& turn keenly away before tracing it all back to that relentless moment.
One could stand & gaze at it but at what corner do you begin
your mend? What else to do but look to Kelli's
the man you adore will soon adore you. Patience, I'm told.
Planets will align. According to her, love for me is on the horizon.
All I've to do is close my eyes, turn my sleepless head into the pillow, forget
how far the horizon was the last time I looked at its ugly, laughing head.

"The Rules"

I

Missy, if he cracks that door again —
even the smallest bit — you be ready
to Karate-Chop it, Rambo the sucker
if you have to. When you're in: take
your coat off, sit your butt on the sofa,
ask for something cool & sweet
for your tongue, bat those eyelashes
fiercely & say, "Oh, Thank you,
brutha, for the invitation . . ."

II

I'm watching my neighbor's turtle, Ertl.
Say it.
　　　When Ertl hears me enter
　　　she knows I'll feed her —
　　　poor thing gets so excited,
　　　swims back & forth, bobs her head.
　　　But as soon as I get within arms' length
　　　she hides.

You're not a turtle. Don't emulate.

Dowser

I have always hoped to marry
an older man, probably once divorced,
who'd appreciate his independence;
some simulation of my father: wise, kind,
patient but forceful. JenLee exclaims: *Young. Young!*
You already move too slow. I concede. Although,
I don't know any young men who are dowsers.
& he will have to be knowing of water's secret.
Like fear, it is always there waiting to be found out.

High School Diary Entry #1

We both like him, are like two hyenas circling prey,
eying each other, readying ourselves for the lunge —
after all, the first one at the meat eats well.
Ain't that how it works? We're marking turf,
the turf is a path, down the path snarls a runaway Mack
with souped-up headlights.

I don't believe single, heterosexual men & women can be
platonic friends. Well, maybe. But one of the sexes,
usually me, is left ass-out, nursing some major crush,
then grudge, then phony-non-chalance thing. Which is to say:

when JenLee explains "every man is either a purpose,
a season, or a lifetime. Don't make a man into a lifetime
when he's only supposed to be a purpose," I think of Jimi
wailing away at that guitar, claiming to be needing some Peace.

So, he says to the audience: *If anyone here can tell me where Peace is,*
come backstage after the show. No one went back there.

Not one person could give him what he wanted.
Truth is, I never want what I need. What I need is often
unextraordinary, a necessity to be endured like underwear
holding everything in place when all I want is to hang
loose, be free. Jimi was probably like that, too.
I bet he'da taken one look at Peace & said, *Oh, hell naw,*
you ugly bastard, slammed the door,
& gone back to all the beautiful racket he was making.

Three days later Jimi was dead. No one knows if he ever found Peace.
Probably did but wouldn't recognize it. Probably held his breath, hoped
it'd go away. Why give up the loose & free for the damned boring?

So here I am, knowing I don't *need* him but knuckleheading
my way into making him a season or even a lifetime. The thing is:
I might never be able to make a man I want into a man I need.
Maybe the best I'll ever do is be able to recognize one from the other.
Maybe all I can hope to do is put my ass in front of a Mack truck,
welcome what comes with wide eyes & call it for what it is.

Sweet,

this is my apology.
You were the roadside boys
I wanted to love. For a decade
I've been holding you at bay. You, loves
lost, big-eyed boys, tender men who offered
so many possibilities that I am fat with them,
take this apology & do not blame yourselves for
I was crafty, turned
when I meant to still.
How many lives have I thrown to the greedy wind
& where have they gone? Here is my story:
down the road a bit — beyond the long trees
reaching for their hot drink —
is an indentation between weeds where I sat
& watched you pass. Beyond that,
a road gaping, full & ugly.
To be in the woods so long is to learn
the wrong language. I believe the trees
finally rustled, "Girl, we understand:
Between anger & madness lives sorrow
but even *we* have had enough. Go home. Go back.
Look to the mirror, she will show you the rest."

But she too would say, *Desire, I lie. I lie.*

Desire

I am so rich my hands dip
with diamonds.
Tonight I am homebound,
waiting on the train.
Desire comes shuffling its ragged ass
down the platform
where there are no bystanders,
no witnesses to say who I was,
what happened here.
When Desire holds me up,
strips & leaves me
so light, so plain & simple,
there will be no recollecting
what my hands held before I peered
into his wiling, murky face.

Faith

After Clifton, for T

The leaves outside my window burn from the outside in
& the days darken quickly, shiver themselves closed.
In the window my reflection is still as the branch &
the spider, who days ago cast her web, waits. Faith,
today, does not show—sends her messengers instead
& they are a ruthless, rowdy bunch. They dive & jive
but I am timid so they chide & gibe, do not offer
to explain. Faith, I am sure, is watching, must feel
there is no reason, just now, that she should bother
showing her face. If you ask again, I would have to say:
Yes, the ground goes to bare, leaves to brown,
puddles & bees to their place, this is how I am,
I am still & I am waiting.

Crushed

This is the lewd drive-by, the moment at night
when birds stop calling, when walls are black as sky
& sleep won't fall but hovers like a bastard. Man,
you are with her & though she'll most likely be dust
you brush off, I cannot sleep through your lovemaking,
imagine it at my front door, not bothering to knock,
just breathing coarsely on the other side.

If Humor were awake, where would she be,
what would she be wearing?
In somebody's pitiful graveyard dressed in drab,
etching, "'Chil, here lays a lonely fool."
What convinced me to say, *I want you to be happy?*
I do not, do not want your hands on her body.
Wanna be dust if only to flitter the air,
fold around your lips & their odd turn.
Wanna snatch Insanity by her coattails
& give the spiteful bitch a whirl.
Wanna be dust, I say. Man, I cannot sleep,
there is too much noise outside my door. Love,
I cannot dream.

Hope

is a hussy & former playmate of mine.
In pigtails & bows she runs around the playground.
Folks ogle, find her cute. They don't see her
flip the bird, show the moon. They don't see her
sweetly prey then suddenly bite or how she sneers & spits,
makes even the blind see blue.

The Shoes

When we're talking & your silences are big
& fat as a butterball turkey, when your eyes cut
& cross from me to the floor like a carving knife,
when you can't hear what I've said (*I need the in between*)
& accuse me of being demanding as a child,
is it like in the mornings when you're standing at the closet,
looking down at those shiny wingtips? I always wonder
why such hesitation, do you fear the mirror?
Is that your heart trembling? Man, is that you I see
with eyes scared of your own shoes?

The Conversation

So here she is, The Conversation,
after all of it, the long months of it,
the tucks & bends our forgetful bodies made,
the arms & grins, the sweet, secret nods.
You sigh & beg, *are we okay?*
Here it is, that moment
when our words, stumbling along
the wall's thin line, plead to be steadied
& grabbed, then offered. We sit
hands under our thighs, watching—friends.
I pause & sigh, *yeah, we're okay.* But, here she is,
that lopsided girl, tripping in front of us, still.
Still.

Crossroad

As a kid I didn't care for the crusts of bread,
would pick them off, pulling until, as Momma said,
all the important stuff was gone.
This was intuitive, my desire. Between us,
between what I know & don't know
lives a canyon, & I sit on its cliff, picking
my fingers. You will not utter what I need
& who knows why. Perhaps you fear the echo,
the bellow of your voice. Perhaps you fear
it'll cause a slide. The canyon grows deeper, each day
a grain goes to a tiny bit of wind, a rain. I slide,
Love. You'd become the crust, your tongue
held all the important stuff. It is something to know this,
to get up from the perch & walk away understanding so little,
trusting only that the sweet, gooey middle was good.

To Do

for Liz

It might be that we think too much, me & these men, each of us
scooting our probes around the corner before we'll take a step —
as if scientists or very cautious beachcombers.

It might be that instead of imagining the catastrophe
that would be my lips once he yawned away, I should
nudge them forward.

Maybe I should treat his butt as if it were an apple. Or,
as I'm a shifter of words, be bold & spit it out.

& what of my heart hiding neatly beneath her clothes?
What will I tell her, that sweet, weeping girl,
how would that conversation go?:

I told you so. I know. I told you so. I know.

The Ex-Boyfriend

Long before those tire-irons & chains got him
I was on the tail end of being dumped.
Ten years have passed
& his legend is the stuff of rancid breath.
When truth suits me: The Ex-Boyfriend did such & so
& I did not move.

Too long these wounds.

I, who appear so resilient, keloid. Fat
pockets of venom bubble every surface.
Whatever man comes sniffing
surely whiffs decay. Even now,
when I can imagine how his mother's eyes must still run
raw, I sometimes forget—joke with friends
who correct my tense: Gone is past.
My tongue learns, has relinquished some venom.
The body, though, remains bubbled.
& I still look to love with lunatic eyes.

We are a conglomeration of memories — some real, many not.
Our task, if we strive to live courageously,
is to examine them rigorously, learn to differentiate one from the other,
recognize the truth in each, & act accordingly.

PART THREE

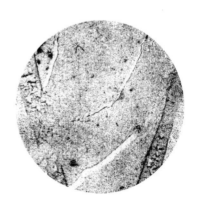

The Story Goes

for The Gumbletons

of the six brothers, two defectors attended her wedding,
along with the Storyteller, who was not family
but might as well have been. The four absent brothers,
did not approve of my black father & later, my black self.
This story told to me in faith explained so much:
the cousins I've never known, the birthday gifts
never received, silence, a family foreign.

After Momma died, I found the material proof,
why her eyes did not beg, *Brothers, but why,*
didn't you love me?: a wedding album. They were there,
the brothers, a roomful of sweet, giggling boys. & yet,

this memory is not mine, might as well be her
slippery, beating heart, it is so quick
through my hands. How to hold it
I do not know. What to say?

How could a story be so wrong, so long in its telling?
No defectors, no Storyteller at the wedding
just the other four boys, their spouses or lovers,
my mother & father, grinning triumphantly
through the lens. The story sighs,
I am the Storyteller's burden.
You might have looked to your mother's eyes.
& they said she loved them all, always.
I thought, despite what they had done. What power.
To be so resonant while whispering. To be so sly.

I think of human lips molding around their stories,
how we cast shadows about, darken them

with our fears as if the evidence will die away, too.
I think of my lovers, how they have been cast
to rid myself of that girl & her ill-fated questions.
How is it, amid so much dissent, you are in the world,
so narrowly loved, so pitched aside? My fears, pulsing
blue & white like water raging or fire against the wick
of a flame, said *No. To bear a love so strong would be to inhabit*
your mother's story, all love twisted away, a lover shriveling
towards death or away in disgust, but gone. Grab here,
along the sides of the easily surrendered.

You are not so strong, girl.

Like my mother's, my eyes never lie. They might beg
& borrow their histories, but gleaming or wet they gossip.
Who now will know my eyes well enough to recognize their evidence?
& if this story had not been told, how would I be —
in the world a bit stronger & with love
doing its bone-dance in light,

in light? I will teach my children to be mindful of lips,
to watch the eyes, for surely I, too, will beg difference with history.
Surely, the world was never as bad, my loves, never as bleak,
the pain or happiness never so red. For, the small girl
without the birthday gift who grew into the woman
long without love's triumphant grin, will subside,
diminish   in fact, but grow stronger in will
& she will rise into her own story & her longings — a story.
& those tales will go, be taken into my children's blood
& that blood will throb beyond recognition
but for the bit of evidence still gleaming in my eyes.
I will tell them to track it down, dig deep,
& believe the good glimmer. *Children,* I will hum,
there goes the Story swinging its soft, slippery head.
Oh World, look to my eyes, look to my eyes, in love & forgive.

ACKNOWLEDGEMENTS

Indebted thanks to the editors of the following publications:

5AM: "Home," "Body Politic," and "You"

Callaloo: "Miscommunication" (as "MFA Meeting: Re: Poet Hire")

Clackamas Literary Review: "Friendly's"

The Electronic Poetry Review: "Sweet"

Ellipsis: "U're Looking More & More Like a Comic Book Hero"

Ms. Magazine: "In Search of an American Language"

Obsidian III: "On Cops & Color" (as "Cop Ing") and "The Others" (as "Jacob's Son")

The Oregonian: "911"

Pleiades: "Benediction" and "On Love & Solitude"

The Potomac Review: "South Carolina: Boone Hall Plantation, 1999"

Rosebud: "On the Collection of Ethnic Memorabilia" and "The Hats"

"In Search of an American Language," "High School Diary Entry #1," and "On the Collection of Ethnic Memorabilia" all appear in *Short Fuse: The Global Anthology of New Fusion Poetry*, editors: Todd Swift and Phil Norton, Rattapallax Press, 2002.

For their kindness and support, heartfelt Thanks to:

Ai, Kenneth Carroll, Ava Chin, Jacqueline Ann Dowdell, Nikki Giovanni, Lisa Glatt, Robert Gumbleton, Yona Harvey, Terrance Hayes, David Hernandez, Marie King, Yusef Komunyaaka, Jeffrey McDaniel, Jo Ann McGreevy, E. Ethelbert Miller, Amanda Pritchard Moore, Robert Morgan, J.C. Todd, and the friends who have been so supportive — and tolerant (ya'll know . . .):

Luv, luv, luv

and gratitude.

— C.

CRYSTAL WILLIAMS, a native of Detroit,
Michigan, is among a generation of writers
for whom assimilation, invented remem-
brance, and cultural responsibility have
become major themes. She is Assistant
Professor of Creative Writing at Reed
College in Portland, Oregon.